The Progressive Mindset of Success

By Nathan Earl

Copyright Nathan Earl © 2017

Other than the quoted text and sayings used in this book, all contents belong to Nathan Earl.

All rights reserved. No part of this book may be reproduced in any form without permission in writing from the author, except in the case of brief quotations embodied in critical articles or reviews.

All quotations are the intellectual property of their original creators.

Basically, if you try to sell, recreate, copy, or otherwise use this book commercially, or distribute freely without permission, you can get in a lot of trouble. All I have to say is, respect my work, and focus on creating your own success. Do NOT resell my work without permission, and we will get along just fine.

NOTE TO READER: This book will only help you if you read it all the way through. You may not agree with everything, or understand everything. That is fine. So long as you read each page, and learn what you can, you will be given the seeds of a mindset that will give you the power to change your life, but *only if you act upon the information you learn!*

TABLE OF CONTENTS

1. Introduction	1
2. Understanding Who You Are	5
A Look Into Your Own Mind	5
3. What A "Successful Mind" Really Is	11
A Look Into A Successful Mind	11
How Do Successful Minds Work?	13
4. Learn To Earn Vs. Earning Without Learning	17
Earning Without Learning	17
Learn To Earn	20
5. Relearn How To Learn	27
How We Are Taught To Learn	27
The "Idle Mindset"	29
You Need To Relearn To Learn	30
"The Progressive Mindset"	33
6. Unlocking Your "Progressive Mindset"	39
Understanding Failure As Opportunity	39
The Positivity In All Failures	42
The Science Of The Mind Towards Success	44
7. Believing In Yourself	49
"Whether You Think You Can, Or You Think You Can't, You're Probably Right!" ~Henry Ford	49
8. Visualizing Your Success	53

Visualize Yourself Working	53
Visualizing Yourself As Successful	58
Time Management:	61
The "Pomodoro Technique"	61
The True Power Of Your Mind	64

9. Goals Are Gold! 67

The Definition Of Goals	67
"Goal Ladder"	70
After Goals Are Set	73
Achieving Daily Goals	75
The Power Of Habits	78

10. Success Is Not An Accident! 81

Self-Empowerment Through Thoughts	82

11. Failure Is The Door To Success 87

12. Now You Know, So Go! 90

You Now Know What You Didn't Know	90
My Parting Words	92

Conclusion 95

Feedback	97
Join Me On My Social Pages!	97

1. Introduction

First off, I want to say thank you for getting this book! Not only is this book literally several years of my studies and experience all compressed into an easy-to-read book, but it is exactly what you need if you truly want to learn what it means to be "successful."

In this book, you are going to learn scientifically proven facts about how people think, why people are successful, and how we are taught to learn the wrong way. However, there is a solution to this, and you will learn that as well! Why else would I write this book for you?

Really quick, let me tell you who I am if you don't already know, and then I will get to what you'll be learning throughout my book.

My name is Nathan Earl. I am a 25-year-old internet marketer and entrepreneurial-minded man. My personal saying is, *"I'm not crazy, I'm motivated!"* Until recently I have stayed "under the radar," simply because I was happy with where I was and what I was doing. That's not the case anymore.

I have created multiple niche-market affiliate sites, in which I make a decent amount of money. I don't like to say numbers, simply because I don't like creating expectations. Maybe someday I will create a "mastermind" group of my top students, with which I will share my earnings and how exactly I achieved those specific numbers, but that's not the point of this book. The point is, I worked hard, stayed focused, and used what you will be learning in this book to achieve my own goals. This book is *exactly* how I achieve my goals!

"To learn about success is to learn who you can become, and what you can do!"

The reason I decided to become a digital product marketer, creator and an author is because lately I have been seeing a growth in the "Internet Marketing" niche, and this isn't always a good thing. Yes, the opportunity is amazing, and you can achieve great income online, but there are too many people selling "get rich quick" schemes, and no one really talks about how to train your mind to be aware of those schemes! This is where I come in.

Before I started generating income, let alone building my first website, I struggled for about two years. I wasn't struggling with building a website. That's honestly the easiest part of working online. The hardest part about becoming successful is learning to think correctly!

My problem was how I was thinking! I wasn't thinking right! I wasn't thinking about who I needed to be, instead, I was focused more on what I had to do, and hated the thought of doing something that I didn't get quick results from. *This is not good*!

You should never put what you want in front of who you need to be in order to get what you want! I will explain more on this later. I simply want to express to you that no, nothing comes easily to anyone. Success isn't a God-given gift to the few "chosen ones."

In fact, if you want to talk about "God-given gifts," look at your mind. Your mind, just like mine, is malleable, transformable. By the end of this book, I hope your mind will be molded and yet freed at the same time.

With that said, open your thoughts, grab a notepad, and let's teach you about your mind.

2. Understanding Who You Are

A Look Into Your Own Mind

First off, who are you? Are you a man who works at a fast food restaurant? Are you a woman who works at the local grocery store? How about a CEO of a major company? Are you a business owner who hit a wall in your business' progress?

Truth is, it doesn't matter who you are. There is only one difference between you and people like Steve Jobs, Bill Gates, Mark Zuckerburg, Oprah, Will Smith, and anyone else you can think of who has achieved "success."

What is this difference? Your *mindset*! Anyone can be successful, regardless of personality type, experiences, etc.

Right now, I want to prove this to you. I'm going to ask you a few simple questions, and you need to answer them honestly. It may even help to write the questions down on a piece of paper, and then leave space for a simple "yes" or "no" answer. You will come back to these answers by the end of this book.

1. "Are you the type of person who enjoys challenging yourself?"
(Answer)

2. "Are you truly happy with what you currently have?"
(Answer)

3. "Are you willing to learn and do what it takes to get what you want out of life?"
(Answer)

If you said "No" to the first 2 questions, but "Yes" to the 3rd, you have what it takes to become successful. I'll explain this shortly. Right now, I just want you to see where your focus is.

If you said "No" to the 3rd question, close this book, go watch a movie, and forget about being successful. I'm not being harsh. I'm being honest. If you are *not* willing to put in real time and effort to first learn, and then act as needed, you will never see success in any aspect of your life. It's a proven fact. Read books about people who have become successful. Read auto-biographies, life stories, journals, and so on of people who have created success and fulfillment with their life. You will see the facts in every single one. It was all about their mindset!

"Without action, there is no progress. Without progress, there are no achievements, and without achievements, there is no success!"

However, like I said, if you said "Yes, No, Yes", in that order, you are more than qualified to take your life into your own hands, and create a successful mindset, followed by a successful life. I need you to write this down really quick though, before we get too deep; "I will pick *one* plan, and *stick with it*!"

There's this thing that people get, and it's called "Shiny Object Syndrome," or "SOS." This is when people start thinking they want to make changes in their life, so they go out and start finding solutions. Then they start one, obviously. Then they find another, so they quit their first one and start over with the new one. And again, they find the latest fad, start that one, and quit their other plan. You see where this is going? *Pick one plan and stick to it*!

The entire reason I asked if you are the type of person to challenge yourself is so *you* would show *yourself* that you won't stop in the face of adversity. Trust me when I say this, "There will be lots of adversity trying to stop you!" Since you don't mind a good challenge, this is nothing new to you. Those who meet challenges face-to-face will also meet success face-to-face.

I have one last question for you. *"Are you the type of person to believe in yourself and your actions, or do you just daydream of your future and never take action to achieve it?"*

The truth is, most people want to be successful. If everyone who wanted something got what they wanted without trying, then why would you even read this book in the first place? It's because that's not how it works! Success is the reward for those who grow internally first, spiritually second, and financially thirdly.

I say spiritually not to convert you to any faith or religion, but to stress that you must believe in a goal beyond your own selfish wants and needs. You need to have an eternal drive to stay focused on what will keep you motivated when you hit walls and roadblocks in your path. Whether it's in a Creator and a higher calling for yourself and your finances, or you dream of helping children with medical problems, or solving world hunger. It's up to you. Just make it huge, and make it burn inside you like a fire that won't be put out for anything!

Now that you are starting to understand who you are, I want you to take a moment and write down three goals, one for each of the categories I just laid out for you.

Example:

Mental: I will unlock my mind to be open and understanding of the purpose and requirements of success, through my focused efforts, along with help from others.

Spiritual: I will create a vision in myself of people who are struggling in an economically unstable world, and use that vision of others' pain to drive me every day towards helping them find peace in their life and with God. (I do not mean to offend, only to give examples.)

Financial: I currently make ($x,xxx/month). I will make ($xx,xxx +/month) in order for myself to be financially free and stable, and have enough to help my family, friends, and others who are in desperate need of my help.

These are simple examples, but they are very close to

exactly what drives me, in case you couldn't make that connection to my goals and my purpose for what I do.

You are, right now, a "normal" person, and you always will be "normal," referring to how your mind works. So is any successful person. They just learned to think differently.

Now that you have a few very basic and simple goals laid out for yourself, let's move on. Next, we will take a look into the minds of successful people.

3. What A "Successful Mind" Really Is

A Look Into A Successful Mind

"Is a successful person willing to challenge themselves?" Yes! Without a challenge, how do they progress?

"Is a successful person ever truly happy with what they have?" No! No matter where they are, they will never settle. Settling leads to laziness, and laziness leads to destruction of progress.

Successful people always try to do a little better with their business, family life, spiritual life, financial life, and fitness. This is not to say that they don't enjoy their life!

They love their life because of what they have created for themselves. They take time to enjoy their rewards, but they also take time to maintain and grow what they have, like gardeners and their flowers.

Once a garden of beautiful flowers has been planted, sweated over, nurtured, grown, and bloomed, the gardener continues to nurture and maintain those beautiful flowers. If the gardener says, "Well, it looks good! I'm done!" the garden would die and slowly become overrun with weeds. Eventually it will completely die off.

It's like lottery winners. About 80% of lottery winners, who are instant multimillionaires, end up broke in a few years. Why? Because they tend to be lazy, uneducated, and selfish. They blew their money without learning about taking care of their finances. Well, guess what. Those people were literally handed financial freedom for the rest of their lives by pure luck, and they threw it away! However, before you judge them too quickly, ask yourself this, if you won the lottery, would you take care of your money, or would you lose your mind and blow it like all the rest?

"Is a successful person willing to learn and do whatever it takes

to create the future they dream of?" Yes! How do I know? Simple. If they weren't willing to learn and act, they wouldn't have become successful in the first place!

Again, their success is the result of growth in their learning, growth in their mindset, growth in their business, growth in their relationships, and, eventually, growth in their income.

How Do Successful Minds Work?

The thing that no one really talks about is how a mind *really* works. Why? Because the mind is so complex, that no one will *ever* completely understand its functionality. It is something only God has a manual to, and only He will ever have, so don't wait around for one!

Although there is no Earthly "Handbook To The Human Mind," there is something close. It would be impossible for me to write it all down, however, I can do my best to simplify what I have learned.

Successful people fail. Does that stop them? No, it doesn't! Why? Because failing makes them realize they are just like everyone else!

Why is it that successful people fail just like everyone

else, and how does that affect them? It's because they literally are *just like everyone else*! The only difference is, when they fail, they see their progress, and comprehend the changes they need to make to better themselves! This is popularly called, "Failing Forward." Find a book on it, and read it!

Successful People Set Goals! How many goals have you set? Most of you at some point have probably said, "This year, I'm going to start going to the gym and lose weight!" or "This year, I'm going to save more money every paycheck!" on New Years, right?

January 1st hits, and you see the gyms completely packed! Trust me, I know! But what is really sad is how few are left after the first two or three weeks. They give up. They feel a little bit of pain and they quit!

So how is it that successful people are "so much stronger" than "normal people" when it comes to pain and trials?

They are not! Look, you need to stop thinking that successful people are super-heroes and start realizing that they are normal people with a different mindset! They have a keen focus, which isn't a born gift. It's not a talent.

"What is it then?!" you ask. It is simply focus. *You*

have focus as well! You are just focusing on the pain and discomfort of working out or saving money. You lose focus when the next "cool thing" comes up. Again, people fail because of "Shiny Object Syndrome!" Successful people do not allow themselves to quit and start something new without first finishing what they started, and they try and fail many times to learn how to get it right.

Successful people focus on the end goal!

I want you to write that down. Just about anything that I bold or put in italics, you should probably write down. Writing things down helps you remember it, and trust me, if you want to change, you need to learn to remember what you read.

Going back to successful peoples' focus, they feel just as much pain when working out as you. They have the same restrictions as you when saving money. They understand that they won't be able to go out to eat every weekend. They wake up with sore, stiff muscles just like you do.

The only thing is, instead of focusing on the pain or lack of instant gratification or pleasures, successful people focus on the end goals. When is the last time *you* started something and finished it?

So, for those of you who agreed with me when I first started this section; you understand and agree with me that we all set those goals at the start of the New Years, and then we lose our focus, our drive, and our motivation, and we just give up. Right?

If you now understand that the only difference between you and the millionaire or professional body builder next to you is the fact that they focus on the end goal, and not the pain of getting there, you can now start making little changes to think more like them!

I will talk more in-depth on this later.

Before we get too crazy with goals and mindsets, I want to teach you a major problem I've found, not only in the world of online business, but in all career/business mindsets I've researched.

4. Learn To Earn vs. Earning Without Learning

Earning Without Learning

So, what exactly is, "Earning Without Learning"? Well, it's exactly what it sounds like. People who start earning without learning will never have a foundation to earn more than they are paid.

An example of this would be working at a fast food restaurant, or a warehouse. Basically, it's just simple, 9-5 jobs.

They do learn, but they only learn what their boss

tells them or whatever they need to know to keep the job and make a paycheck. Prove me wrong if I am, but how many people do you know who work these kinds of jobs can go and start a business or work in a CEO position based on the basic knowledge they were trained for at that job? See my point?

Of course, do not confuse this with getting a raise in payments or position. Let's say you work at a fast food restaurant. You start out as a cashier taking orders. You take a month to learn that position.

After a few months, you pick up on what your managers do, and they notice that you do an excellent job with what you were tasked to do, and that you are helping your coworkers. They may even give you a raise and teach you to be a manager. However, that is *all* they teach you.

They will not teach you what the CEO of that company does, how he or she works, what he or she must do, or anything. Why? Because they don't need you! They already have *hundreds* if not *thousands* of people all fighting for that next raise! They can kick you out the door, drop you flat on your face, left to drown in bills without a paycheck and not blink twice at you. Ever see employees demand pay raises? They get replaced by someone who will gladly do the same amount of work for less pay just so they can pay the bills.

This is the struggle of earning without learning. Now you need to go out, find another job, and your new employer will pay you while you learn what you need to do to keep that job.

This is the J.O.B., or Just Over Broke Cycle. 99% of you know what I'm talking about, and trust me, I know it sucks!

Final words on Earning without Learning; if you don't take extra time to learn a set of skills and grow your mindset, you will never be free of this J.O.B. Cycle, which is the nightmare of reality. Find a mentor, build relationships, and learn a solid skillset.

I cannot stress enough how important it is for you to learn skills, grow mentally, and fight for what you deserve. When you figure out what you want, and start fighting for it, others will see that, and you will build relationships with others to help you get where you want to go.

Let's take a look at what it is to Learn To Earn.

Learn To Earn

This is where it's at! Remember me talking about the CEO of that fast food company you work for? Do you think he or she really started as a cashier and worked his or her way to the top by being good at what people tell him to be good at? NO!

Let's say Bob is a CEO; if he just did what people told him to do, he would never have risen above the status quo. He never would have stood out from the crowd, and never would have learned the skills he needed to operate a business and take charge of the people under him through leadership and business skills. Outside education and support are key to rising above the status quo.

People who are leaders obtained these skills either through college or self-education. Yes, it is possible to make a lot of money in the corporate world without a college degree or a lot of experience. All it takes is stepping up to bat, and proving to a business that you can knock out a home-run for them. Once you have worked for this business a few years, you can use that on a resume to get a higher paying job, and again, prove your skills to them, etc. Build a solid support-group through friends and positive relationships, and you will obtain even more power to take your success to the next level.

Example:

An example of this is Steven Spielberg. He was originally turned down by his first college attempt at University of Southern California.

He then tried again at California State University. He majored in English. *English!* I know loads of people who have majored in English, and the best J.O.B. they get is a school teacher. I am not talking down on school teachers whatsoever, because I have a very high respect for them and what they do daily. My mother and her mother were both school teachers. They sacrifice a lot of time and frustration to give children tools for a good future.

However, one of the most successful men in movie creation and directing was an English major. His dream was to be a movie director. Remember, having an English degree does almost nothing towards the corporate world of movie directing. There is a degree for that.

While he was in school, he became an unpaid intern at Universal Studios. He did this out of his willingness to learn what it takes to achieve his dreams. He studied everything he could while he could.

While he was working in the editing office, he was given a chance to create a short film for the company. He created *Amblin'*, and the producers absolutely loved it!

Long story short, he stepped up his game, learned what he wanted to learn, as well as what he needed to learn, and when the opportunity arose, he jumped on it. He had one chance, so he took it without question and proved to the film studios that he had what it took to be a director and script writer. I'm sure the English skills helped with script writing. He used his knowledge to achieve his dream.

From there, he continued to work toward his dreams and hone his skills. Today, he is one of the most successful film makers in history. Why? Because he was *focused on the end results*! He didn't let the pain of missing paychecks or difficult studying deter his dreams!

By learning the skills you need in order to create the future you want, you will be able to work little by little towards your end goal.

Remember those three goals I had you write down?

What would keep you from fighting for those goals? If your goal is to make $10,000, or $100,000 per month, would you let someone get in your face, tell you, "You can't do that! It won't work!" and quit? Or will you say, "I'll prove you wrong!" and never give up on your dreams?

Now look, just because you are going to be learning to earn more money, doesn't mean you can't earn while you are learning.

With what I do, as far as my online business, I started out learning first. Just like you are doing, I read books. I bought courses. I studied my butt off. The only thing is, I did it on my spare time from my day job. To this day, I still read books as often as possible and learn more every day. Will I ever stop learning? No! If I stop learning, I stop creating, I lose. Period.

I worked a demanding job, and sometimes I would be gone for a week or two at a time. Even though I wasn't home, I had my laptop, and you can bet that I took my laptop with me. If I had Wi-Fi, I was researching how to be successful, how to build websites, how coding worked, how marketing worked, how to write, what works, what doesn't, how to be a leader, how to build solid relationships, etc.

If I didn't have an internet connection, I was reading a book that I would bring with me. Usually I would bring a book that teaches successful mindsets (go figure), marketing techniques, becoming a leader, creating productive relationships, and anything else about entrepreneurship that I could get my hands on. The funny thing is, I *hated* reading! Ask my Mom. I drove her nuts as a young child not wanting to read anything. Now I love it!

Reading stories was different from reading on how to change my life, though. I got so excited about learning, that I became an absolute nerd about internet income streams, passive income, marketing, becoming a leader, building relationships, learning how to teach, and anything else I could do through the internet.

And that's earning while you learn! Not only was my job paying, and paying me decently, but I was building a business while I learned. As my websites took shape and I wrote content, I started to see results after a few months! It took a while, but after about 6 months, I was making a few extra dollars a month, on top of my job! Not bad for a 20-year-old kid!

The point that I am trying to get across to you is it doesn't matter what you learn, so long as you start learning something! Steven Spielberg was an English major! If he would have listened to what everyone else was saying, he would have become an English teacher making just $20,000-$40,000/year, depending on where he taught. Now he has so much money he could build an entire University that teaches how to film and direct movies, and he could pay the staff a $100,000/year salary!

I'm not trying to digress or fill this book with "fluff." I'm trying to get you to open your mind, see the facts, and learn what I am laying out for you. You can learn, and as you learn, implement what you learn in your work, and you *will* see results as you work, so long as you *stay focused on the end results of your efforts*! This way of thinking is true for all goals. If you want to lose weight, *stay focused*! If you want to better your relationship, *stay focused!*

If you ever need a visual of someone getting you to "get your head in the game" and focus, look up "Dwayne Johnson – Focus!" on YouTube. It's entertaining and helpful when you need that little "boost" to focus your energy.

Next, I want to talk about *how we learned to learn*. I

want you to relearn how to learn to earn. But how exactly are you supposed to relearn how to learn in the first place? Confused yet? I was. Don't worry, I'll explain this in the next chapter.

5. Relearn How To Learn

How We Are Taught To Learn

If you went to public school, you know what this feels like; *"Okay kids, today, we are going to be learning about the relation between ectoplasm and blah blah blah alsdkjfdasgasdghjasdf…" Who cares*!? Unless you were really interested in the anatomy of amoeba cells, you probably didn't care! If you were interested, good for you!

We were forced to learn with a generic, unfocused, standardized, copy-and-paste mindset. Open the textbook, find this fact, write about it, and then brain-dump it because it wasn't important to us.

Again, we all need this! We all need to be taught the basics, because without being exposed to the variety of topics in public school, we would have never learned the basic skills and understanding of the world we were about to enter.

My problem is that once we learn all the basics that we are required to learn, we are *never* taught how to *truly learn for ourselves*! This is "Self-Education."

We are only taught to learn what someone asks us to, but as soon as we try to study something on our own, we get lost, frustrated, confused, and quit. Am I wrong? It's difficult.

Most people don't know how to pay attention, and when they do, and they start seeing progress, they quit at the first roadblock! They get bored and say, "Screw this, I'm going to go enjoy myself." People would rather feel instant pleasure than create a progressive lifestyle.

This is because they feel that they "aren't good enough," or that they "weren't born for these skills," or whatever stupid excuse people have polluted their minds with. Our minds! We are all guilty of thinking lowly of our own capabilities! You just need to prove yourself wrong!

To sum up how we were taught to learn; we were taught through criticism, and that people are born with different talents, skills, and abilities. *False*!

This is called an "Idle Mindset". The "Idle Mindset" simply is static; non-progressive.

The "Idle Mindset"

The Idle Mindset is that if you can't do something, or you are incapable of something, or fail at any given situation, that you were meant for something else, and need to accept that. The Idle Mindset is an absolute abomination, a denial of creativity, independence, and progression.

"If you are good at something and win, then you are a winner. If you try something and fail, then you are a loser, and that is all you will be." This is the Idle Mindset. It is a poison to the human mind, and therefore 99% of people either fail or never even try to be successful!

Yes, people are born with talents, but mostly, people are born with interests. These talents and interests are the seeds of greatness instilled in our minds at a young age.

If you want to talk about "God-given gifts," this is it. What we truly want to aspire to be. The only question is, will you push yourself to achieve your dreams, or will you let people tell you how to live?

You Need To Relearn To Learn

Is that sentence confusing? It shouldn't be. It's a completely correct statement, and here's why; you need to relearn how to learn!

"So, Nathan, if I have been programmed my whole life to learn this way, how am I going to reprogram a life's worth of programming to be successful and self-educating?"

Does that question pretty much sum up what you're thinking right now? If it does, GOOD! We are getting somewhere. In all honesty, I am holding your hand as you reprogram yourself right now. By reading this book, you are self-educating. You are forcing yourself to grow mentally with the end purpose of growing physically, spiritually, and/or financially. Right?

By opening your mind and accepting this information positively, with a goal of learning, you are learning right now.

Here is exactly how you will be learning from here on out, in everything you do, in all aspects of your life, and for the rest of your life;

Learn from positive experience through failure!

Write that down, because if anything out of this book, that is the one sentence that will change your life forever, if you take it to heart, and act on it!

Here's an example of how this works;

You practice martial arts. You have trained for over a year, but have never been in a competition, because you didn't think you were ready.

The day comes, and you enter your first competition. You have devoted a year's worth of energy, studies, blood, sweat, tears, joy, pain, and frustration for this one day.

You get to your first match, and you have been so anxious to test your abilities. Your coach gets you pumped up and focused for the fight, and you see your family cheering for you in the crowd.

The match starts, you take a few hits, land a few hits, get the taste for a good fight, and BAM! You get high-kicked in the dome and you're out like a light.

So, what do you do now?

You just got whooped on, even though you worked so hard for this test of your abilities! Do you quit, or do you train harder? Do you go back and study what your opponent did, or do you go cry about it and give up?

If you take the positive experience of what happened by understanding that you have the ability to stand your ground, but your opponent was simply stronger, or quicker, you understand what you need to work on! Analyze your strategy, as well as your opponents.

By creating a positive experience through reflection on a failure, you will not only understand yourself and your abilities in a deeper level, but you will also know where to focus more of your energy in training. This is called "fortifying a weakness." If a boat has a hole, you patch it up, right? However, you should put most of your energy into what you are already good at.

This applies to working online, a brick-and-mortar business, family, marriage, working out, and anything else you learn. It doesn't matter what area it is in, only that you learn what happened, why it happened, and how you can improve on it.

I want you to think about something in your past that you have worked hard for, and then it smacked you back in the face and you felt like you failed. I'm not trying to bring back bad, painful memories, but I am trying to get you to see that the fault isn't in your ability to learn, but in your lack of progression.

This is the "Progressive Mindset."

"The Progressive Mindset"

The "Progressive Mindset" is the exact opposite of the "Idle Mindset." You learn through failures, trials, errors, mistakes, successes, others' errors and mistakes, and so on with positive experiences. You learn by challenging your skills and knowledge, pushing until you fail, and learning the next piece of information until you pass the challenge. You do this over and over again. You now have no limits!

The Progressive Mindset is your new mindset from here on out. I want you to write that down.

You are now no longer in an "Idle Mindset," but in a "Progressive Mindset."

As you learn, you test your abilities. As your abilities fail, your efforts become stronger and more focused. You push harder in the areas you need to strengthen to overcome that next obstacle.

Let's take your new Progressive Mindset back to that martial arts competition in our new example.

Instead of going home and pouting that you're a loser, and that you suck, and that you're going to quit, you go back to the Dojo. You go up to your trainer and ask them what your opponent did that you didn't see coming.

Your trainer says that you never practiced blocking a high-kick like you should have. Instead of focusing on defense as much as offense, you just focused on kicking someone's butt! That's the cool part, right?

So, long story short, you go and spend another 2 months learning the defensive skills you needed, but you didn't know you needed.

Notice this! You don't know what you don't know! You can't beat yourself up for failing due to a reason that you couldn't help! If you fail because you didn't know about it, who cares!? Learn from it, go back, and do it again, and again, and again, *and again 'til you get it right*! Once you beat your challenge, push yourself again! Rinse and repeat! Never stop!

Back to the fight. You go up against the same guy from last time. Guess what, he's sitting there smiling knowing all he has to do to is a high-kick, knock you in the head, and he wins. Right? Because he thinks he's a winner! He thinks he is better than you! He thinks with an "Idle Mindset!" Right? Because he has already achieved something, and never failed, he already thinks he's better than you! His "Idle Mindset" tells him what he already knows, and not what he doesn't know! His idle mind hasn't expanded its skills and knowledge for the upcoming task, or trial, at hand.

This is where you see the "Progressive Mindset" blow the "Idle Mindset" out of the water!

So, this kid thinks he's going to kick your butt again, easy win for him, right?

The match starts, and right off the bat, he throws a quick jab to distract you, and then kicks high, laughing, knowing that he has you in the bag!

Little does he know you have a progressive mindset, meaning you went back, learned from your failure, made a positive adjustment to your skills, and learned his tricks of the game.

Soon as that high-kick comes for your head, you easily glance his shine over your head with your right forearm, and with the same fluid motion, you low-kick his grounded leg out from underneath him.

He slams to the ground, head first. This guy, who started the match laughing, goes crawling off the mat crying with a nice headache. You won.

Moral of the story: People who think with an "Idle Mindset" limit themselves. There are no limitations on your life except for the ones you put on yourself!

A person who learns to think with a "Progressive Mindset" will not only become better in any and every aspect as a person with an "idle mindset", but they will become successful. They will not be defeated by anything, because they find pleasure in being better than they were yesterday! Creating progress also creates attention and eventually a following!

A progressive thinker fails, just like everyone else. However, unlike everyone else, a progressive thinker will always win in the end, because they learn from experience, and move on, working every day possible to be better than they were. People will take notice of this. This is a good thing, because in all honesty there is no such thing as "solo-success."

Really quick, I want you to know this; no matter how hard you work, focus your daily tasks, and read books on success, you will never reach your full potential alone. You need support, assistance, mentors, and leaders who you can create relationships with. Without people, your efforts are wasted, because to become great, you need more energy and abilities than one person can muster.

Now that you understand what a "Progressive Mindset" is, in the next chapter, I will teach you how to truly unlock this in yourself, so you can reap your well-deserved rewards for your efforts.

It will take time, it will take practice, and it will take consistency. This is true for all things that eventually lead to success. Before you can achieve true success in all your life goals, however, you *must* learn how to think progressively.

6. Unlocking Your "Progressive Mindset"

Understanding Failure As Opportunity

In order for you to unlock your "Progressive Mindset," you must understand that failure is not failing in itself. Failure is a door for you to open, and then enter, in order to learn the next step for you to become successful.

I want you to write down the following:

"I will work hard to achieve every single goal I set. I will not focus on the pain and trials of the path to my goals, but I will focus only on the goals' end

results. If I fail, I will not complain, but instead, I will study the cause of failure. I will create a positive experience through the failure. I will learn from my lack of understanding to create an understanding, and with understanding, I will work hard to succeed where I once failed. At any point that I fail, I will remember; Failure is an opportunity to learn from experience in order to create success!"

This almost made me cry while writing it. Why? Because I struggled so hard with this in my past that I nearly quit. I wouldn't be who I am, have what I have, or be where I am today if it weren't for this paragraph that I wrote out two years ago.

I am not a shrink, nor have I ever studied in-depth the process of creating a new mindset. I simply fought failure until I reached success. This paragraph is how I did it, and if you take this to heart, put it on your wall, and read it every day, you will understand why it changed my life. It will change yours as well, so long as you stand by it, follow it, and believe in it, but most importantly, believe in yourself!

A quick story about myself;

I used to give up. A lot. I gave up so much, that instead of building a website and working towards my dreams, working out, and talking to my family, I sat in my bedroom and played video games and watched movies, just like most people my age.

I gave up on everything. I gained more weight than I ever have in my life. I lost motivation. I got mad when I daydreamed about being successful because I thought it would never happen.

Then one day, I got so mad at myself, that I told myself, "I'll show you! I'll prove you wrong! I have the skills I need! I know what to do! I'm not afraid! I'm going to just do it and see what happens, and you're going to see what you are capable of! *Just do it!*"

I built a website. I spent 30 days writing articles, adding content and products, and driving visitors to my site. I started working out before I wrote articles, every day. Working out helped me energize and refresh my mind to write content and be creative.

After 90 days, I had about 300 monthly visitors, and made 1-3 sales a month through an affiliate website. Then, after 6 months total, my car payment was being paid for by my website. Before I knew it, I has making decent money. *Never lose focus, never stop giving 100% effort!*

The Positivity In All Failures

There is a thing to be said about positivity in failure; it's hard to find!

Usually when people fail, they are frustrated, angry, depressed, annoyed, self-conscious, self-judgmental, irritated, and ready to rip someone's head off! Right? Seriously. You've failed at something. You can relate!

The thing is, that isn't what separates successful people from unsuccessful people. Successful people feel all of these emotions just the same as unsuccessful people. However, they get over it, and they reflect on *why* they failed.

Instead of going to your friends and family and moping around about how you failed, go to your office. Calm yourself down. Read a book, go for a run, go lifting, say a prayer, meditate, whatever you need to do to find yourself, gather your thoughts, and focus with rational thinking.

Remember, you are now a progressive thinker! You're not an idle thinker anymore! You're better than that! You think about your future, not your past! You're not going to allow yourself to stoop so low as to give up and be just another body that someone pays to make themselves rich through your work!

If you are one of those few people who focus their efforts through anger or aggressive thinking, because I know this is a real thing for some people, you need to focus that aggressive energy towards productivity instead of destruction.

You can do it physically, or mentally. I either work out, or, I read 'til I fall asleep. Why do I read out of anger? I don't act out of anger often at all, but by reading, I am feeding my unsettled mind with information to show myself that I can do better if I focus on positive actions.

This is a trick I have also used with some of my close friends who get angry easily. Just give yourself something to do to burn off the energy, as well as assure yourself that you are capable of what is at hand.

However, if you can calm yourself down quickly, then it will be easier to find the positivity in a failure.

This is how I am now. Instead of getting frustrated, I get curious. When I do something wrong, I say to myself, "well, that sucks. I didn't know about that. Guess I have some more learning to do." Simple as that. I just see what I need to learn, and get to it.

Again, "You don't know what you don't know." You can't be mad at yourself for not knowing something that caused you to hit a roadblock or failure.

The last thing I want to say about this, in all honesty, is there's no such thing as failures. Failure is giving up completely. You only hit "speed-bumps" from now on. You have no more failures.

The Science Of The Mind Towards Success

Are you starting to think differently? Are you starting to realize how you currently think? Like I said, this is a science. It isn't a magical spell for people to rain success upon their pretty little heads.

I'm not going to get into the people who say, "You only get rich if you sell your soul to the devil!" Look, I have my own beliefs and faith. To each his own. If you respect me for who I am, then you have mutual respect from me. I am trying to teach "hard work pays off."

I do not want people saying that the only real key to

success is to do something so drastic as selling your soul. The reason I'm saying this is because I was just asked if I did this in an email.

No! I changed my mindset and created positive relationships with influential people to boost my authority as a leader, as well as gain mentors for my success as a product creator, author, and leader. That's it. Instead of being greedy, selfish, and negative towards the speed-bumps in my life, I changed my outlook towards challenges and problems.

I keep mentioning relationships and mentors throughout this book. You should probably take note and find multiple mentors, people who have succeeded in the areas you wish to succeed in, and learn all you can from either their content, or content about them! Without people, followers, mentors, leaders under and above you, you will struggle greatly to reach your potential for success.

Just as I am teaching you, there is a science to the human mind. The more you use your mind in a certain way, the more neural pathways you create by pushing neurons to that part of your brain.

For example, artists, even though they may be

naturally talented, learn to be more creative, and learn to add more definition to their art. They hone their skills.

I used to airbrush and paint. I wasn't an 8-year-old prodigy. I was interested in painting, and so I started out drawing. My sketches as a kid were horrific! You could hardly tell what they were until I was in junior high school!

I started watching art videos, drawing lessons, how different mediums effected their results, etc. I just started learning, is all I did. I learned, and I put what I learned to action. Slowly over time, I developed the ability to not only draw what I pictured in my mind, but I could paint as well.

I started a small painting business after high school, and I made a lot of money with it. Again, this goes back to two things you've learned already; "learning to earn" and "progressive mindset."

I learned a skill set, and my parents were paying money for that. I wasn't making anything. After a few years, I put it to use, and a few local people saw what I could do. They asked if I could do some work for them, and they paid me handsomely for it!

This was possible, because I continued to grow the

neural pathways throughout the parts of my brain that conduct creative ability by practicing. **Practicing and consistency are key!**

When you build up skills through practice, and you consistently progress your skills, you start to believe in yourself. You believe in your "talents", and your skills. You believe that you are now capable of doing more than you were in the past.

Through believing in yourself, you will become unstoppable.

7. Believing In Yourself

"Whether You Think You Can, Or You Think You Can't, You're Probably Right!"
~Henry Ford

Enough said, right?

No one ever reaches success by doubting themselves! Seriously, think about it. Would a man build a successful empire if he continued to tell himself, "You can't really do that. You're a nobody. You have no special skills. You aren't a leader."

No! Only people who believe in themselves will be

successful. This goes back to the "Progressive Mindset!"

You must have a progressive mindset in order to believe in yourself and overcome your trials!

Are you starting to see how successful people think? You should! In this one book, I have put down over three years of studying notes, theories, systems, scientific facts, and motivational speakers.

Believe me, I wouldn't have written this book if I didn't believe in myself! It's hard, time consuming, and somewhat frustrating at points. Have you ever heard of writer's block? It's a speed-bump I have, just like every other author! Do I stop? NO! I go out and learn what kind of message I am trying to teach, study it until I understand it, and turn it into something that you, as my reader, can implement in your life, and I truly hope I make an impact for you!

I don't allow speed bumps to stop me! I refuse to give up on something that could change someone's life. If this book only changes one person's life, then my goal is achieved. I simply believe in myself and stay focused to change peoples' lives for the better.

Can you see where everything you've learned is starting to come into play? People are so baffled at the successful person's mind, and so intrigued by the "mystery," that they never focus on improving their own mind.

Turns out, it's not that hard to create a successful mindset! You just need to stop getting distracted, and focus! **FOCUS!**

Again, as I mentioned earlier, if you want an image of how I am yelling "Focus," watch a video of Dwayne "The Rock" Johnson called "Focus," on YouTube.com. It is a comical video that helps me not only focus, but get a good laugh sometimes. Disclaimer, I am not affiliated or associated with Dwayne Johnson in any way. I just find it an entertaining way of someone who is successful reminding people of their goals and to focus up. He also helps people *believe in themselves! Go figure!*

"Without belief, there is no faith, without faith, there is no future."

If you don't start believing in yourself and having faith in your ability to learn, you won't have the future you want. Period.

It will literally be impossible for you to create success, let alone achieve a simple goal, if you do not believe in yourself.

If you want something simple, easy to remember, but effective, you can write down the following;

"Believing Is Achieving!"

One of my most motivational and inspirational authors ever is Napoleon Hill. In his book, *"Think And Grow Rich,"* he has a saying that has stuck with me since I read it;

"Whatever the mind can Conceive and Believe, it can Achieve." ~Napoleon Hill, *Think And Grow Rich*

Simple as that. Only when you start believing in not only yourself, but your ability to achieve your goals, you will start to see results, and even find success.

The easiest way to start believing in yourself and your goals is to visualize yourself after you've met success!

You need to visualize not only *doing* what you need to do to be successful, but you need to visualize yourself *being* successful! This leads us to our next chapter.

8. Visualizing Your Success

Visualize Yourself Working

The first part of visualizing success is to see yourself doing what it is you need to do. In order to act on an idea, you need to visualize in your mind exactly what you need to do, before you take action. This isn't to say that you need to spend hours planning! Spend five to 15 minutes of planning for every hour of working. This will prevent you from wasting valuable time.

An example of this would be a baseball player. Think of how baseball coaches tell their players to "Focus on the ball. Visualize its path to you. See the ball coming, but recognize when to swing. Picture yourself swinging hard, contacting the ball, and sending it into the stands for a home-run!"

This is a form of visualization. This is one of the most important and underestimated powers of your mind. Truth is, the ball travels from the pitcher's hand to the catcher's glove in literally the blink of an eye. The human mind is so much more powerful than we realize.

Many people are taught to focus on the end goals, and this is not wrong by any means. However, from my studies, there seems to be a lack in visualizing the action of achieving a goal. You should never jump into action blindly, without a plan, and without visualizing a course of action, with a determined result in mind!

For myself, I would literally sit down with a blank piece of paper and a pencil. Whatever it is I was wanting to do, say for instance, write this book; I would create a mind-map, outline, and layout. This is also how I build websites. I draw out the basics of what I want before I start building. I also plan a workout routine before I start lifting.

The reason for this is because I now have a vision of

what I want. I'm not lost for ideas. I have a solid focus on a predetermined plan. This prevents me from feeling "stuck," or not knowing what to do with myself. This also prevents me from wasting valuable time, which is *huge*!

Now, I want you to do a little mental exercise.

Pull out your notepad that you have been taking notes on, or the one you should be taking notes on. Now I want you to read the following, and then write out a scenario, similar to what I just did with the baseball example.

What is it that you want to achieve? Just like the baseball player, he wanted a home-run. What do you want? To be fit? To make more money? To have a better marriage? Anything. Write down what you want.

Now, I want you to visualize your path to that goal. If you are wanting to make more money, will you work online? Work harder at your job? Whatever it is, write it down.

Finally, I want you to visualize yourself doing exactly what you need to do to achieve that end goal. Write down a paragraph of the steps you could possibly take to reach that goal.

You should have a goal, a path to that goal, and a plan of action to achieve that goal. It's not that hard, is it?

But now, ask yourself this; how many times have you *really* done this to achieve something in your life? Probably not many. Most people just don't do this. They just think they know how to do it, so they "wing it."

The point is to step into action only after you have considered a path to follow, steps to take, and a goal to reach through those actions.

Right now, I don't want you to imagine yourself just jumping to a CEO position, on vacation, sitting at the beach, and drinking margaritas. I want you to visualize what it takes to get to that CEO position.

This is difficult for a lot of people, because when they think of work, they think of sacrifice to their enjoyment in life, and painful, as well as numbing tasks that seem to never end. We all do this, and it's normal. That is, it's normal for people who haven't learned to *think progressively*! It's a good thing you think progressively now!

Remember that idle mindset? Instead of thinking about how they will progress to achieve a goal, people with an idle mindset think about how much it sucks getting up at 6:00 AM to go do the same old stupid job they hate, or to go for a run because it hurts!

Who cares what it's like right now?! The point is to

progress! Focus on what you can do to get out of not only the "Idle Mindset," but out of those same old tasks! If you don't learn to think with the "Progressive Mindset," then you are in an idle mindset, and that idle mindset will pin you to exactly what you don't enjoy in life, because you will never focus on bettering yourself. You will only focus how much you hate where you are, and how moving forward hurts!

There is an old curse that an Asian culture used to say to someone they didn't like, and it is this; "May you never leave from where you are now." OUCH! Think about it. May you never move forward, progress, travel and adventure, grow successfully, nothing. Just waste away where you are. The sad truth is most people today passively waste away in their daily lives. My one wish for you reading this is that you progress in your life daily!

Visualize the things you need to do. This does not mean that your plan must be perfect! No plan is "*perfect*." The best plan is, "A plan to take action." Things will change, problems will arise, and goals may be achieved sooner than originally visualized, or later. It's the randomness of life!

So long as you think progressively, believe in yourself,

visualize yourself working and achieving goals, you will make major changes in your life.

Speaking of life changes, most people get motivation through thinking about the end goals. Mine was and still is to help my family by making more money. I wanted to be able to own myself, my life, and to treat my parents and family for everything they've done for me. Not only that, but to offer more to people who have nothing and no one to give them a hand. People can always use love and support, no matter where they are in life.

This brings us to creating motivation through *visualizing yourself as successful!*

Visualizing Yourself As Successful

Now that you understand the basics of *visualization*, and how this is extremely powerful for taking accurate action towards goals, let's learn how we can use visualization to create powerful motivation to complete the tasks we have planned.

First off, I want to bring up a matter that seems to be a debate between success coaches.

Depending on the coach, some will say that

"Daydreaming" is a waste of time. They say that if you are daydreaming, you aren't working, and if you aren't working, you aren't going to be successful.

On the other hand, some coaches say that without Daydreaming, you lack inspiration and imagination, and without inspiration and imagination, you cannot visualize yourself as successful, which in turn prevents you from creating success through your conceived visions.

Before I give you what I think, I'm going to give you a lesson that changed my life forever. When you are laying down to go to bed, picture yourself sitting down in your comfy recliner, in your beautiful living room, with your epic-sized flat screen. The TV show that you turn on, is the show called "The Future You."

As you watch this TV show, you see yourself living the life of your dreams. You can taste the food you see yourself eating. You can feel the body that you worked hard for. You can see all the people you've helped with your success. You can hear the fountain in your mansion's backyard. The very touch of your new silk bed covers is a sense of ecstasy.

The point is, you get sucked into the TV show and you create the life you truly want. You mold your entire mind and all your senses around this vision of your future. Since your subconscious can't decipher reality from imagination, it reminds you daily of that memory of your success. This will drive you to think about success daily and create a burning sensation to put in the effort and focus necessary in order to get what you crave so desperately!

The more you do this, and I suggest doing it every night before you go to bed, not only will you become more positive about your future, but you will create a clearer image of it. This was a technique I learned a long time ago, and in all honesty, it changed my life, because I could see the life I wanted! **Do this technique every night!**

So what's my honest opinion on "daydreaming"? Daydreaming is awesome, but don't do it while you work! Other than picturing the future life I wanted before bed, I found that for myself, if I work for about 25 minutes, and then take a 5-10-minute break, I can use my break to think about how awesome I will feel knowing that I achieved my life goals.

Some of you may ask, "Why only work for 25 minutes and then take a short break?"

Time Management:

This is called the **"Pomodoro Technique"**.

You can research this more in-depth for time management, which is extremely important. Without time management, you lose track of time. When you lose track of time, you lose track of your actions, which in turn, results in the loss of your future success.

I am not an expert in time management, so this is going to be a shorter section. This does not mean it's not important! Educate yourself on time management by reading a book or two on it! I learned the "Pomodoro Technique" through an entire book.

However, I am going to give you the simplified version, which seems to work extremely well for not only myself, but for everyone I have coached personally.

The "Pomodoro Technique"

The Pomodoro Technique is a time management technique that uses a timer. Set an alarm or a counter-top timer for 25 minutes. During this time, focus 100% on the task at hand. When the alarm goes off, set it for 5 minutes. Relax. Stretch. Take a break. When the 5 minutes is up, reset it for another 25 minutes, focus up, and get back to work. Do this as many times as you wish, and as long as you can to achieve the most progress every day without overexerting yourself.

During these 25 minutes, do not allow yourself to get distracted. Put 110% focus into the task at hand. Silence your phone, close the door, close the window, do whatever you need to do to free yourself from distractions.

Then spend about 3-5 minutes *visualizing* what you are going to do. There it is again! Visualizing is key.

Set up a plan of action, set a goal you want to meet by the end of the 25 minutes, set the timer, and get to it! Work your butt off, and stay completely focused until that timer goes off. Don't even look at the timer! *Just work*!

You won't believe how much you can get done before that timer goes off. Honestly, once I started doing this, I was blown away at how quickly that time flies when you are putting in some serious work! That is progress! You're thinking progressively, you are building a progressive mindset, and you are creating results through progress in your work!

Are you starting to see the "Progressive Mindset" take shape in your mind? It's easy to create success when you are handed a handbook on thinking! Thinking is the only difference between your current life and your future success. Don't forget that!

Going back to creating motivation, I didn't go down a rabbit hole on the "Pomodoro Technique" on accident.

There is an exact purpose in what I write, and how I write it. By introducing you to the concept of visualizing yourself as successful and switching suddenly to a time-management technique, your mind will automatically connect visualization, a sense of pleasure through achieving success, and a time-management technique.

Now, you're probably thinking, "Well that's really dumb." But is it? I have studied the basics of association in the mind through neuro-linguistic programming. You don't need to change the font sizes, or have a change in your voice for an idea to stick like many believe, if you know what I'm talking about.

The easiest way to make something stick in a person's mind is to talk about it in a way that creates a sense of self-accomplishment, such as an in-depth story, or something that creates a sense of pleasure in the audience.

When you visualize yourself being rich, happy, in shape, working from home, and with a happy family, you feel good about yourself, and it's even better knowing you achieved that life through managing your time and staying focused on goals.

I believe the Pomodoro Technique should stick now. If it doesn't, let me know. Then again, if you remember it later and think to yourself "I don't think of it often." then my work is done, because it is embedded in your mind, whether you use it or not.

The True Power of Your Mind

Your subconscious mind hardly forgets anything. When you visualize yourself being successful and happy with everything you have achieved, it will often give you the actual feeling of happiness you're working for.

It doesn't matter if you truly felt this emotion, or just imagined to the best of your ability how good it will feel, your subconscious mind will remember that sense of enjoyment. When it lacks enjoyment, it will remind you of that feeling, memory, or *daydream.*

Since you have connected the technique of visualization with a sense of pleasure and enjoyment, along with a method of time-management that will help you achieve that reality, your mind will remind you of all these associated memories, and you'll remember what to do to make those dreams reality.

Now all you must do is act when your mind urges you to feel good about yourself! You're welcome.

I never enjoy beating the living snot out of a dead horse, but now that that's over, let's do a fun little exercise;

Go back to your main goals that you wrote down. Now, all I want you to do is close your eyes and imagine exactly how you would act and feel after achieving those goals in your life. Picture yourself as the successful you in the future. Now look back at all the hard work you've put in through your time-managed actions and plans. It feels good, doesn't it? Trust me when I say this, "It feels better when it's real!" This is your *motivation*!

Also, a quick note for Time Management:

Spend a few days as you normally would, only throughout the day write down what you have spent your time doing, and how much time you've been doing it for.

If you watched TV for 3 hours, write it down! If you spent 2 hours playing video games, or watching YouTube videos, write it down. Same for staring at your phone, or Facebook.

The point is see where you are using your time in the day. You have 24 hours in a day to become successful; nothing more, nothing less. All people are blessed with the exact amount of time in a day. Successful people use their time more wisely than unsuccessful people. The more time you waste, the more time you add to the time it'll take to become successful! Don't forget, time is the one thing you can never get back. Don't waste it!

Once you realize where your time is being spent, fix it. You will become more motivated to work more as you see major progress throughout the days. This is a huge part of self-motivation. Simply seeing results as you go! Now, focus that time on achieving goals!

Don't forget, however, no matter how much time you put into your work, you will need to remain patient! "Good things come to those who wait." Or is it, "work wisely with the time you have"? Don't expect to become rich within a month! Stay dedicated and it will pay off!

9. Goals Are Gold!

The Definition Of Goals

Most of you know what "goals" are. Most of you also know that goals are how people achieve success in all areas of life. You also know that goals can be made to achieve anything through a set path and plan of action.

The sad thing is, 99% of people *never reach their long-term goals!*

What is a goal exactly? The solid definition:

"Goal: The object of a person's ambition or effort; an aim or a desired result."

If you go to Google.com and type in, "Goal definition," this is exactly what you'll see. That, and how points are made in soccer and hockey, but that's not important right now.

What is important is the staggering fact that just about every single person in the history of the world has set at least one goal, and most of them never reached it!

Here's an example. Again, going back to January 1st. How many people are at the gym? *Tons*! How many are at the gym in February? About half as many. How about in June? A quarter of the people that originally started! 75-90% of the people at the gym are the same people who were at the gym in June last year. This is because they set a goal and are focused, dedicated, and *patient*!

Of all the people who quit, they all had a goal to get in shape, and yet they let pain, frustration, discomfort, and impatience rip them away from their dreams of being fit!

People today crave instant gratification! When they do something, they don't want to do it for long. They just want the end result! I've even heard of people getting frustrated over their food warming up in the microwave! Are you kidding me!? You put in a frozen meal and in 5 minutes you have a hot meal ready to eat! You're getting hot food quicker than any other generation *in history*! You should be thankful it only takes 5 minutes, and not an hour to cook a meal! (By the way, please don't live off microwaved food. Eat healthy.)

And yet people get frustrated over that. No wonder only 1% of people are successful. It's because they understand that pain, discomfort, frustration, and self-doubt are temporary! What they want is something far greater; **PERMANENT RESULTS!**

By pushing through all the bad that only lasts a little while, they achieve enjoyment of permanent results. If those people at the gym would just make a lifestyle change to work out daily, every day, forever, they would never be out of shape again. They would enjoy success in their health! They would never feel bad about their fitness again! It's a permanent change they can enjoy forever! The thing is, you can't stop! *Nurture your success*!

The same goes for saving money! Save a set amount every paycheck, and you'll have money!

This is how you need to think when you set a goal;

"Is this goal obtainable with my current situation?" If it is not achievable in a 3-6-month range, make it a long-term

goal, and then break it down into smaller steps.

By breaking one main goal into smaller steps, and those steps into smaller steps, you will create a "Goal Ladder".

"Goal Ladder"

A "Goal Ladder" is a set of goals in an order from quickly achievable to long-term achievable.

This is a method I created for myself in order to visualize what I need to focus on next. Go figure, I said visualize again! Anyways, a "goal ladder" looks somewhat like this:

1 Year

- Earn $xxx,xxx more than last year.
- Be stronger and faster than last year.

Monthly

- Make $x,xxx More than last month.
- Build 1 new website/product.
- Add 10% weight to last months max weights in the gym.

Daily

- Lift(healthy lifestyle) for 2 hours, run 2 miles.

- Work(business and income) on websites/products for 4 hours.
- Read(self-improve) for 3 hours.
- Study(self-educate) for 3 hours.
- Clean(appreciation for my home and rewards from success) for 1 hour
- Spend time with family and relaxing(spiritual/mental health) for 5 hours.
- Sleep(recuperating needed energy for tomorrow's work) for 6 hours.

You get the idea. This is just a quick example, and it's not perfect for everyone, but you can see how I broke my one long-term goal into several smaller steps.

You notice how I have easy, simple, and small daily tasks? These add up to what I wanted to achieve by the next month, and then my monthly goals lead into my yearly goals, and so on.

You can get a giant white board, like I have, and start on the right side, either top or bottom doesn't matter, and create a "stair-like" set of goals.

Start with what you want far out, and make it 2-3

HUGE goals. So big that you could die happy if you reached these goals.

I think that making $500,000/year in 5 years would make most of you happy! Or turning your marriage around in 1 year! Or donating $1,000,000 in 5 years to a children's hospital! Whatever it is, whatever is bigger than yourself, and will drive you, write it down.

Then, step back, usually about half the time length, (Years to 1 year, to 6 months, to 3 months, to 1 month, to 2 weeks, to 1 week, to daily. This is how mine is set up) and work your way down in time periods.

Your daily goals should almost be a schedule, like I showed in my example. And yes, you shouldn't waste time by sleeping more than 6-7 hours a night. I don't anymore, and trust me, it's easy to get used to when you're changing your life!

In my example, I also want you to go back and look at what I put in parenthesis. They are all major factors of my life, my values, and my focus. You NEED to do this as well, or else you will simply blow off "daily tasks," or "daily goals."

After Goals Are Set

Now that you have your goals laid out, or you will have your goals laid out, preferably on a whiteboard in your office, kitchen, or bedroom, you need to think about why people fail, and how you can avoid failure. Remember, "failing" is only a speed-bump to you now!

You know why people fail, right? Because they don't feel good doing little tasks! They don't feel good after working out and getting sore! They don't feel good because they can't go out on the weekends and waste their money on beer, food, and movies!

You know what hurts more than those? Failing at life. Yup, I said it. If you fail at life, no one in your bloodline will remember you, and none of your family members' lives will be changed for the better.

Even just the thought of being a nobody and a failure should put a fire under your butt so quick that you jump up and start **visualizing** what you need to do to change that!

Are you getting it now!?

Now that you have goals, *visualize how good it will feel to be successful through your actions*!

If I could sound like Rocky Balboa, I would use his voice for this. *"Let me tell you something you already know. The world ain't all sunshine and rainbows. It's a very mean and nasty place, and I don't care how tough you are, it will beat you to your knees and keep you there permanently if you let it! You, me, or nobody is going to hit as hard as life, but it ain't about how hard you hit! It's about how hard you can get hit, and keep moving forward! How much you can take, and keep moving forward! THAT'S HOW WINNIN' IS DONE!"*

It's almost like Rocky knew about having a "Progressive Mindset," and mastered it. Don't you think?

So, how do you fight back at life and take what you're worth? You visualize a progressive course of action towards your goals, how good it will be to achieve those goals, and believing you can achieve those goals. Then, start knocking out your simple, easy, doable daily goals.

If you complete every goal, no matter how big or small, over one month, you can turn your life around.

You need to create a habit for achieving daily success.

Achieving Daily Goals

When you start achieving daily goals, they start adding up, but this takes a change in habit, just like I mentioned.

I once heard a saying, and I'm going to share that with you. Just like everything else I put in bold and quotes, you should probably write it down for reference later. Or just read this book again, it's up to you;

"Anyone can do anything for 30 days. If a man forces himself into a new positive habit daily, after 30 days, he will have replaced a negative habit with a positive habit. After 60 days, it is a part of his daily lifestyle. Successful people create permanent habits that makes becoming successful an easy lifestyle!"

This is truth. This is fact. Going back to the people at the gym, most people don't last 30 days. Honestly, most people don't last a week. Why? Because that first week, your body is screaming, "Oh *@#& no! That hurts! I don't want you to do that anymore! We aren't doing this anymore! You feel okay being out of shape. If you don't feel pain, you're okay! Stop working out!"

Well guess what, your body just told you to quit. Your mind is trained for enjoyment, remember? When it feels pain, it reminds you of enjoyment, and makes you focus on that!

You need to own your mind, and tell it to shut up and deal with it for 30 days! It will learn to like it, and when it learns to like it, it will remind you, "Hey! I need my endorphins for the day! Get your butt to the gym and get a pump on so we can feel good! Your new body is starting to look great, but it can look better! Get on it!"

By talking about how your mind reminds you, you should also remember the answer to this question:

"What is the technique we talked for time management, and how does it work?"

Bam! I'm willing to bet you said, "The technique that starts with a P, and I work for 25 minutes with 100% focus, then take a 5-minute break, and do it again!"

Unless you remember the word, *"Pomodoro"*, you won't know the name. The only thing that matters is that you remember how it works, and how effective it is.

Now, implement the "Pomodoro Technique" with your daily goals. Again, BAM! Mind blown!

Look, surely by now you see what the inside of a

successful mind is like. It's beautiful insanity. To a normal person, it looks complex and extreme. To the successful person, it looks like a normal life built out of persistence of habits.

But it works!

The reason that "Goals Are Gold," is that without goals, you don't visualize success, and without visualizing yourself as successful, you are not motivated, and without motivation, you don't learn new skills, and if you don't learn new skills, you don't believe in yourself or take action. You just sit there in the idle mindset, wasting away.

I can tie everything you've learned up until this point together in 101 ways, or more. Why? Because they are the true keys to success. They are irreplaceable, but all interchangeable in order.

So long as you use everything you have learned up until this point, and use it daily, you will see your life change in as little as a few weeks to a few months.

Remember! **Whatever you decide to do, *stick with it for at least 30 days*!**

If you need help with this, I will have an automated 30-day "Success Coaching System," which you can use.

Find it at my website when its ready, or subscribe to my newsletter to be notified with its official launch:

https://NathanEarl.com/Success-Coaching

By breaking major goals into small, easy-to-do daily tasks, you will naturally achieve goals through repetition of smaller daily goals.

This then becomes a habit. The power of habits is absolutely astonishing when you really think about it.

The Power Of Habits

When you have a habit, you do it naturally every day. Whether it is a bad habit, or a good habit, your brain naturally guides you to do it every day.

Most people have more bad habits than good habits, in all honesty. This isn't to say that they all smoke, drink, have negative addictions, etc. It just means that their habits include watching too much TV, or spending too much time on their phone or internet without purpose, or even a habit of sleeping too much.

By sticking to these habits, where is your life heading? Is it a good place, or not so good?

Anyone can change habits. You simply need to

replace a bad habit with a good habit, such as replacing sugary drinks and junk food with natural tea, fruit, lean meats and veggies. It's not the fact that you *can't* do it, it's just that you really *don't* want to! When you want something bad enough, you'll find a way to do it.

To create a new habit, or replace a bad habit, you need to dedicate to forcing yourself to make that change, every day, for 30 days. My "30-Day Success Coaching System" will help you do this by reminding you every day of the goals you set, purpose for the goals, your "oath to dedication," as well as daily motivation and inspiration from myself. It will also make you look at your "daily tasks", and remind you how those should be valuable and important to you.

Do not sit *idle*! Putting the "idle mindset" into action is just "going with the flow." You go through your life a day at a time without thinking about values, without effort towards progression, without a vision of your future. Do not let your habits develop through an idle mindset, which will lead to an uneventful, unsuccessful life!

10. Success Is NOT An Accident!

How is that people become successful? I'm sure by now, you probably have a much better understanding of this question, and yet, you probably still have a hint of doubt in the back of your mind that you can be successful in your life goals. Am I wrong? I honestly hope I am wrong, and that you feel motivation and inspiration pumping throughout your entire body!

We all have this little devil on our shoulder that keeps saying, "You can't do that. You're not good enough. You'll never be good enough! Just give up and stick with what you have. It's better than nothing!"

Well, I'm here to tell you that you can tell the Angel

on the other shoulder to go kick that devil's butt for talking to you like that! How do you do that exactly?

You empower your positivity towards yourself, which in turn makes your Angel grow a little more and more, the more often you think positively and progressively, until one day, your Angel gets so buff that he walks over to the other shoulder and literally kicks that pain-in-the-butt devil off your shoulder.

I'm not trying to use religion as motivation, because I understand that some of you just aren't religious, and that's your choice. It is just an image you can use anytime you hear a negative voice in your head towards yourself, as well as your success.

As soon as you start thinking negatively, destructively, or belittled, think of your Angel smacking that devil right in the face and saying, "That's enough! You have no power to hold us back from achieving our goals!"

Successful people don't "luck out" and become successful by accident. They think their way to success!

Self-Empowerment Through Thoughts

A huge key for success is exactly what I just talked

about. By imagining the positive, good energy defeating the negative, not only can you come up with a little cartoon in your head that can make you chuckle at yourself, but you begin to see that you control your mind, and when you can control your mind, you can control your actions, and then the outcome of those actions.

When you think about something, you focus on it. However, there's more to it. When you focus on something, it causes your mind to naturally steer towards that action or result. If you waste your thoughts on negativity, inactive pastimes, and deconstructive habits, you are creating the negativity in your life.

When you focus on the opposite, however, you become positive, constructive, and active, which leads to progression in achieving small goals. Then, after you start seeing little results towards small goals, the results become exponential.

This is how people become successful. They think positively and take action towards any achievable goal within a time period. Most successful people start out taking very small steps. This will create a purposeful life through habits and values.

Once they start to see results, it will get them excited.

They begin to enjoy doing more in the day. They sleep less than 8-9 hours. They only sleep 6 hours to recover the needed energy to put in another 18 hours in the day towards their goals.

When you go to bed, you need to be thinking, "Okay, I have 6 hours to sleep. When I wake up, I need to get as much done tomorrow as I possibly can because my life depends on it! If I sit idle, I will never change, and I will die disappointed with my life and with all things I never accomplished." That, and don't forget to spend some time watching the TV show, "The Future You" in your head before falling asleep!

This should put a fire in your gut for when you wake up. You don't want to waste your years and never achieve all those things you've been visualizing!

A successful man on his death bed will look back and say, *"I am pleased with my achievements. I did good by me and my family. I have no regrets. I fought the best I could to better their lives as well as enjoy my own."*

An unsuccessful man on his death bed will look back and say, *"I don't want to die! There's so much left that I want to do! So many things I need to take care of! Oh God, please give me more time to fix the things I need to!"*

Do you see the difference? A successful person knows they did the best they could every day, and there's nothing more in life they could have done. Someone who didn't set goals to grow and enjoy their life will regret not doing so.

This all goes back to right now. The exact minute you are reading this. Are you going to read this book, and say that it was good, but not take action? Are you going to start setting goals, breaking them down, and using positive thinking to build a "Progressive Mindset" towards achieving goals?

I know for a fact some of you will say yes, but not do it. Why? Because of *fear of failure!*

11. Failure Is The Door To Success

Everyone fears something. The reason most people are scared, or *fear* something is because of the unknown outcome of actions.

Straight honest truth; ***"There is no illusion greater than fear."*** ~Lao Tzu

What does that mean? It means that we literally create an outcome in our head that would hurt us, and we make it more important than the reason to do something! It's that stupid, and yet *everyone does it*! What is the biggest fear of anyone who sets goals? **FAILURE!**

People *fear* failure, because it hurts. It doesn't feel

good. It makes us feel like we aren't good enough, or that we don't deserve what we were trying to get. And yet, other people are good enough? Are you saying people aren't created equally? That people are successful because they are fearless?

NO! People are not fearless. Successful people have fears just like you! The only difference, is they welcome failure with open arms. Failure teaches them to succeed.

Why do they do this? Because through failure, they learn what works, and what doesn't work. You can fail at something 100 times, but it only takes that one time to get something right, and it will change your life!

It's like when Thomas Edison was asked how he felt about all of his failures; *"I did not fail. I just found 10,000 ways that didn't work."*

I'm not saying go out and purposely fail 10,000 different ways to create one perfect way to achieve what you want! That's not the point. The point is, Thomas Edison never let the fear of failing stop him, because he knew that the *one time* he got it right, he would change humanity and civilization forever. And he did!

Your mindset should be similar, only you don't need to change the future for everyone, unless that truly is a goal of yours. Some people do say that how much you earn is the reflection of how many people you help. Looking from a business standpoint, this is correct.

Goals aren't only for money, however, and never should your focus be on money to have more money. Set positive, effective, life-changing goals for not only your self needs or wants, but for others as well. Just remember that whatever you are fighting for, you are going to have fears of failing. To overcome these fears, simply make the reason to succeed larger than your illusion of fear!

12. Now You Know, SO GO!

You Now Know What You Didn't Know

Does this sound familiar? It should. The entire reason you fail is simply because you didn't know something. This is also most likely the reason you bought my book in the first place, is it not? Maybe this book was a gift. Either way, it has value if used!

The fact that you didn't know something didn't stop you.

This may be why you got my book; "to learn what you didn't know in order to take positive, progressive action toward your goals in life."

Tell me I'm wrong if you can. The reason I know this is because a few years ago, I was in your exact shoes. Something was holding me back. I didn't know what it was. Because of this, I went out in search for answers.

Finally, I found out that it was simply, in itself, the idea of "I didn't know what I didn't know." It's mind-boggling, really. We search for answers not knowing when we will find the answer, because in reality, we didn't know what question to ask in the first place!

THE PROGRESSIVE MINDSET OF SUCCESS

Like I've said, the mind of a successful person is beautiful insanity. Some may agree, some may disagree, but once you understand something, you can act on it. Once you can act on something, it becomes easier. Now place exactly what I just said over "Becoming Successful." Once you understand becoming successful, you can act on it, and it becomes easier.

I find it astonishing how many people are looking for the answers that will make them successful, but "becoming successful" isn't possible. It's just not. You literally cannot jump into action in the direction of "success." If you do this, you will lose your mind, because you are only acting without learning. Again, you've learned about this. It doesn't turn out well.

The *action* of "becoming successful", is the *result* of the following (write this down!);

"Understand yourself and how you think.

Relearn how to learn skills for yourself.

Create a Progressive Mindset as you learn through failing, and take actions towards strengthening your weaknesses.

Believe in your abilities and expand them through strengthening your skills and knowledge.

Visualize your success through creating progressive habits.

Achieve goals through those habits.

Never stop."

Look. If that last list doesn't open your mind to the reality that you were just handed the Golden Key to your life's success, I don't know what else to write that will help you.

I can always expand on topics, subjects, areas, ideas, and choices that will help you grow, but until you understand the foundation of success through progressive habits, thoughts, and actions, I can't help you.

Truth of the matter is, I can teach you anything and everything I know, every day, for 3 years straight, but until you learn to motivate yourself, and find the strength in yourself, and to grow by yourself, you will never find success.

My Parting Words

Never give up on your dreams. Never let anyone take your dreams from you. Never tell yourself you aren't capable of achieving your dreams. Let your dreams remind you of what you must do, so that your dreams can become your reality.

It wasn't easy for me. It's still not "easy" for me. Granted, it's easier for me than some of you, simply because I've already learned to create habits that I just naturally do that cause me to make progress every day. I don't have to force myself to do them anymore which, in a way, makes it easier. You can get to this point too.

That doesn't mean that life backs down. Life will forever be going chest-to-chest with you. It will spit in your face and tell you to sit down before you get smacked down. You just need to understand that life is the energy that God gave you. You were not created to be a slave to the masses. You were not created to be belittled, abused, suppressed, and destroyed.

You were created with the life energy to create, fulfill, and assist. Create positive and progressive habits that will lead you to success in all areas of your life. Fulfill your dreams according to what you conceived and believed could become real through your visions. Then assist those who are struggling like you were.

"If you are going to become successful, take as many people with you as you can!" I honestly can't remember where I first heard that, but the point is, don't do this for yourself. When you tell life to get out of your way, and give you what you deserve through your efforts, tell it to let your friends by too!

And lastly, thank yourself. Tell yourself thank you when you do something right. When you reach a goal, treat yourself, but don't spoil your work. Create a positive conclusion to every trial in your life. You will learn to love life, and be thankful for every moment, as this is who you are, and who you will become.

Stay strong, study hard, work hard, progress daily, stay focused, and stay persistent.

Conclusion

First off, I just want to say, "Thank You!" Not only for reading through my book, but for deciding to learn anything you can about changing your life. I know it's hard, but you can do it!

It doesn't matter where you start, so long as you just START! And now, not only did you start my book, but you finished it! That is a huge step in the right direction! You'd be surprised at how many people will start a book and never finish it.

At least, I hope you finished it, and didn't just skip straight down to the bottom to see if there was anything juicy. Well, if you read my book, you should have already gotten more juicy information than any other standard book.

At this point, I would like to ask you for your feedback! Not only does your feedback help me revise this entire book and add to it, but it helps many others who read this book after you! Your input, questions, and ideas could literally be the few words that changes someone's life through my book, and you wouldn't even think that it was possible.

Feedback

To give me feedback on this book, as well as join in my community of readers, you can simply go to the following link and create a free account to comment;

Https://NathanEarl.com

If you would like to subscribe to my daily newsletter with more techniques, training, motivation, and education, please subscribe at:

https://NathanEarl.com/Subscribe

Again, thank you, and I look forward to seeing you in our community for becoming successful, as well as helping others along the way!

Nathan Earl

"I'm not crazy, I'm motivated!"

Join me on my Social Pages!

https://NathanEarl.com/
Facebook.com/NathanEarlOfficial
Instagram.com/NathanEarlOfficial
Twitter.com/TheNathanEarl

Made in the USA
San Bernardino, CA
21 July 2017